The philosophy and musings of a Lincolnshire binman.

IVAN GOSLETT

Copyright © 2024 by Ivan Goslett.

All rights reserved. No portion of this book may be copied or reproduced in any form, whether by electronic or mechanical means, including information storage and retrieval systems, except by a reviewer who can quote brief excerpts in a review.

First paperback edition August 2024.

ISBN: 9798335642439

Imprint: Independently published

Printed in Great Britain by Amazon.

When I discover who I am, then I will be free – Ralp Ellison.[1]

Contents

1. Have you ever considered being a binman?
2. Societal chains.
3. Children love bin lorries.
4. Discovering wisdom from the depths of black bins.
5. Encountering generosity in a self-centred society.
6. Indra's Net.
7. The Duality of Existence: Creation's Two Faces.
8. Keep your phone switched on.
9. Mindful Driving: Appreciating Our Furry and Feathered Companions.
10. Cheers to Recycling: Exploring the Relationship Between Alcohol and Blue Bins.
11. Beauty in God's creation – and lessons they teach us.
12. Waste is simply waste; it's all the same.
13. Navigating the Streets with Dyspraxia.
14. References.

Preface

The inspiration for this book came when I realised how diverse perspectives on life can be. I had always assumed that people generally viewed binmen as rough and uneducated. I could offer a unique perspective on our world as a philosophy, ethics, and theology student. It's important to note that everything written here is my opinion. No one precisely knows the absolute truth, so we learn by listening to the views of others, whether they are right or wrong.

Working as a waste disposal operator in the West Lindsey district, I have had the privilege of collaborating with colleagues who bring years of experience and wisdom to the job. This book would not have been possible without their support and shared encounters. I am also eternally grateful to my wife, who provided a sounding board for my experiences and helped me see things from different perspectives.

Lastly, thank you, the reader, for choosing this book. I hope you enjoy reading it as much as I did writing it.

Chapter 1

Have you ever considered being a binman?

'If we don't change, we don't grow. If we don't grow, we aren't really living'.

Anatole France [2]

Upon completing my first year of studies at a university in Lincoln, my wife and I grappled with concerns about our limited financial resources and the viability of my continuing education. Being a mature student, my decisions significantly impacted my wife, and we often found ourselves in a markedly different situation compared to my much younger classmates. Unlike them, we didn't have the luxury of turning to supportive parents for financial aid as we pursued our dreams. Complicating matters further was that our closest relatives resided in Leeds, West Yorkshire, necessitating our separation from familiar support networks. However, despite these challenges, my wife and I made the deliberate decision to relocate so that I could study philosophy, theology, and ethics at university.

I was nervous about going out to find work at the time. Finding temporary work and being middle-aged is also challenging. Understandably, potential employers would want staff for the long haul, staff who were going to stick around. When studying and looking for part-time work, you inadvertently tell a prospective boss: 'I am available to work, but I'm not staying as I have my mind fixed on something else'. So, my wife and I looked at local work, and after numerous unsuccessful applications, I decided to approach an agency in Gainsborough. They were lovely people and allowed me to explain my unique situation and challenges. After hearing me out, the agency manager asked me: 'Have you ever considered being a binman? I looked at my wife and said, 'Why not?'. I did not go away to think things over or ask family and friends what they thought about the idea. I just said: 'Why not?'

Thinking back on that day, you could say I had a gut feeling; something told me inside that this was what I should be doing. So I agreed to start work the following week. A few days later, I completed my induction, and then later in the morning, I went out to my waste collection round in Nettleham.

You may think a person studying philosophy, theology and ethics is intelligent. Well, this life has different kinds of brilliance, and I was in no way prepared for my first day as a binman. It's not as if I could turn to my professor of ethics and ask him what to expect from this new career path. I was still determining what to expect from this new adventure. And, of course, I did not ask important questions before I started. I thought, point me at the first bin; this will be easy. It is not like I was working in an office environment, with exact tea breaks and toilet facilities. I never even asked where binmen went when they needed the toilet. You can't precisely rap on a door in North Kelsey and ask the householder if you can use their lavatory. That simply will not be tolerated in North Kelsey. And after climbing in the cab of my first bin lorry and introducing myself to the driver, I was not going to ask: 'Where do we go when we need the toilet?' A disproportionate number of words have been spent talking about toilets, so I need to move on with the story of my first shift.

I must admit that I have not spent much time watching binman activities in my lifetime. On this day, I wished that I had paid closer attention. I thought this was going to be a breeze. How hard can it be to collect and position a bin at the rear of a bin lorry? I was about to find out soon what was involved, and since that first shift, I have developed a newfound respect for binmen. In his wisdom, our supervisor paired me with a fellow carrier over thirty years my junior. I was thinking, no problem, I am sure I can keep up with him. My colleague must have wondered why he was having someone old enough to be his father forced on him. This was going to be one long afternoon for him. I guess he regretted coming to work that day. But me being me, I was going to give it my best shot and do my best not to let the team down. My pride would not allow me to admit I could not do this. Have you ever seen a greyhound exit the starting gate at the dog races? Well, my younger colleague had more than enough energy for both of us, and he left me standing, looking for parking. I think around the third street, I was bent over sucking air. I can't imagine what was going through my workmate's mind. Maybe he thought he was not going home that night, as we would still be collecting bins around Nettleham till the early hours of Friday morning.

Whatever he thought, he did not once complain or criticize me. He took his foot off the gas a bit and allowed me to try and keep up. Something I still need to mention is my size. My wife, always so lovely and diplomatic, calls me cuddly. Others might say 'fat'. This particular day, I regretted all the burgers and cheesecake slices I had eaten. How I did not have my first heart attack, nobody knows. I didn't want to overestimate or underestimate my efforts that day, but I lasted about ninety minutes before my body told me I couldn't continue.

I don't think my brain was functioning correctly due to my exhaustion. Therefore, I'm not entirely sure of the exact time I stopped. I decided to put my pride in my pocket and ask the driver and my fellow carrier if I could sit a bit in the cab. They were both excellent and agreed to let me spend some time in the cab. It's also important to note that I had not brought any food or drinks on my first shift. The driver, whom I've grown very fond of since that first day, stopped at the nearest shop and got me a bottle of water. I could embellish this story and tell how I pulled myself together, got back out there, and finished my shift. But that is not what happened on my first day.

I spent the rest of the shift in the cabin, catching my breath. The young carrier took it on his shoulders to do all the remaining work, and the driver helped him with this. I was too tired to think of it at the time, as I just wanted this nightmare to end. I recall how they finished the rest of the shift without my help, and neither complained. When we got back to the depot at the end of the shift, as far as I know, they did not complain to management either since I was asked to come back for another shift.

As the months passed, I found myself increasingly grateful for the opportunity to work alongside some of the most genuinely kind-hearted men one could hope to meet. Society often encourages us to judge based on appearances, but delving deeper into the lives of these individuals has been nothing short of enlightening. Each encounter has revealed layers of depth and warmth that have truly enriched my life, a blessing for which I am profoundly thankful. Getting to know these men on a personal level has been a revelation. Their generosity, camaraderie, and genuine concern for others have left an indelible mark on my heart. They've shown me the true meaning of friendship and service, qualities that transcend societal stereotypes.

So, dear reader, I ask: Have you ever considered the noble profession of a binman? If you have a passion for the outdoors, a desire to improve your fitness, a yearning to contribute to your community, or simply a longing to forge meaningful connections, perhaps this unconventional path might hold unexpected fulfilment and joy for you, too.

Chapter 2
Societal chains.

'Man is born free, yet everywhere he is in chains'.

Jean – Jacques Rousseau [3]

One of the things I have noticed on my travels around Lincolnshire is the inequality in wealth. I have worked in the suburbs, where the streets are so tight, it is almost impossible for our driver to navigate his lorry between the parked cars. I have collected waste at some mansions, where we could park our whole fleet of bin lorries and have room to spare. I can still recall the first time I collected waste in Burton by Lincolnshire; it was a warm and clear summer day. I stood on the narrow pavement, looking at the large home before me. It was magnificent. I must have been standing a bit too long gawking, as our driver had to lean out of his cab window and remind me that we had a job. Our driver did not enjoy the Friday shift, as he had some complicated estates to navigate around Lincoln. But it was my favourite, as we always ended our shift going downhill in Burton. Although I have seen so much social inequality, it was also a reminder that wherever our job took us for the day, everybody had garbage that needed collecting. To a binman, a blue bin is just a blue bin, and the bins in Spridlington are no better than those in Newtoft.

However, one often wonders how such inequality came about. Nearly three hundred years ago, the people of France found themselves in a similar situation of social disparity. The aristocracy and the Church enjoyed immense wealth and privilege, living comfortably in their opulent estates and ivory-clad towers. At the same time, most of the population, the poorer class, struggled to survive in harsh conditions. During this period of extreme social imbalance, a young Swiss philosopher named Jean-Jacques Rousseau made a significant impact by addressing these issues head-on. Rousseau critically examined the roots of social inequality and articulated his ideas in a way that challenged the established order. He famously posited that the problem began when the first man fenced off a piece of land for himself and declared, "This is mine." According to Rousseau, claiming private property marked the beginning of social inequality.

This concept of property fundamentally altered human relationships and societal structures. The notion that lands and resources could be owned by individuals rather than shared among the community introduced competition and division. Before long, more people followed suit, staking claims to pieces of land and erecting fences to define ownership. These physical barriers symbolized and reinforced social divisions as individuals and families began to live side by side with fences between them, literally and metaphorically.

Rousseau's ideas were revolutionary because they challenged the legitimacy of the social and economic systems that upheld the aristocracy's and the Church's power. He argued that the emergence of private property led to the development of laws and governments designed to protect the interests of the property owners, thereby institutionalizing inequality. This critique resonated with many suffering under the weight of oppressive social structures and contributed to the growing discontent that eventually fuelled revolutionary movements.

We only have to think about the way some of the European nations went about colonizing the world. Before we interfered, the Native American Indians, the Bushmen of sub–Saharan Africa, and the Aborigines of Australia would have been free to roam their lands. Bushmen used to roam around Southern Africa, probably going where their food supply took them. They were small communities that worked together and shared resources. As a people, they did what was innate to them, worked together, and cared for one another, viewing each member as equal and valuable. But we, the so-called civilized nations, came along, stuck a flag in the ground, and took what was not ours in the first place. If the native inhabitants did not like it, then they were shot and driven away. And when these lovely new houses became too big to clean, we journeyed out to find the very natives we sent packing, enslaved them with great big chains, and brought them home to spit and polish our homesteads. As Rousseau rightly pointed out, 'man is born free, yet everywhere he is in chains.'

What I find compelling, though, when I admire some of the houses I see daily is that I cannot help but also feel sorry for their homeowners. I often wonder whether these householders, too, are in chains. You will sometimes find a lovely three-bedroom detached house built on St. Giles Estate, with a Tesla parked on the drive, but no one is home. If I were to ask the owners whether they believed they felt shackled, they would probably laugh at me. They could rightly point out that they owned their home, had a nice car to drive, and had takeaways three times a week (more about this later). However, philosophizing about it, one could argue that they are slaves to a consumerist society. When both parents have no choice but to work five days a week and have not got the freedom to take every day as it comes, are they truly free? When we turn around and see what our neighbour has, and we need something bigger and better, the only ones who stand to profit are those who sell us these so-called necessities. I cannot imagine bushmen in huts of different sizes. And if one Bushman had a bigger hut than his friends, they would have to tear theirs down and build an even bigger one for themselves. This would have made the lifestyle of hunting and gathering almost impossible as they roamed from one region to another.

What about a society where everyone has the same size house? On our Tuesday round, we had to cover a few of the smaller villages off the A15, also known as Ermine Street. It may surprise how many large houses are called 'the rectory' or 'the old rectory.' We were always curious because they are often some of the biggest houses. When chatting in the cab, we discuss the irony of these big homes, possibly having a single clergyman as the sole occupant. Was there not a congregant back in the day, maybe a single mother having to raise seven children in a tiny pokey home on the opposite side of town. It reflects how religious and social structures often perpetuated poverty and inequality, benefiting the few at the expense of the many. Moreover, she was probably required to tithe to the Church so that the priest could eat his dauphinoise potatoes and roasted pheasant, along with his glass of Pinot Grigio.

I find it curious that the clergy needed these elaborate buildings to live in when they claim to follow Jesus, who once said: 'Foxes have dens, and birds have nests. But the Son of Man doesn't have a place to call his own' (Contemporary Bible, Matthew 8:20). Jesus' words highlight living simply and without attachment to material possessions.

This serves as a powerful reminder of the contrast between religious teachings and the actions of many spiritual leaders throughout history. I could never understand why religious leaders who were so convinced that they were going to heaven needed to have the most prominent house in the village here and now. What is the point? When we close our eyes for the last time in this life, there is nothing we can take away with us. Whether it is a big six-bedroom detached mansion or a metal shack in a squatter camp, we leave everything behind. The fact that the Egyptian rulers used to bury their possessions with them is a testament to the foolishness of wanting to use our belongings in the next life. Archaeologists have been uncovering Egyptian trinkets for decades; they remain here, albeit now covered in rust.

Contradictions were also present during the colonial era. Priests often accompanied soldiers during the conquest and occupation of lands, justifying their actions by claiming it was all done in the name of

God. Before the arrival of colonizers, the indigenous peoples lived in harmony with each other and the natural environment. They believed that no individual could own land, as they saw it as belonging to no one and everyone simultaneously. These communities lived without emphasizing material possessions, relying on the Earth to provide for their daily necessities. Their way of life was deeply interconnected with the natural world, taking only what was essential for their immediate needs and ensuring sustainability. Upon the arrival of colonizers, we imposed our beliefs and practices in the name of our God, deeming the indigenous peoples uncivilized and in need of enlightenment. We dismissed their spiritual beliefs and practices as primitive, failing to recognize the profound wisdom and harmony they embodied. The indigenous peoples' spiritual understanding of the divine was often far more profound and integrated with their daily lives and the environment than ours. This raises the question of whether our actions were genuinely justified or if we overlooked a more prosperous, more harmonious way of life that was, in many ways, more spiritually enlightened than our own.

Observing that we encounter ancient wisdom embedded in various cultures wherever we travel is fascinating. Despite these societies ' geographical and cultural distances, this wisdom often manifests in similar themes and practices. The ancient Chinese philosopher and prophet Lao-tzu spoke the following words nearly 2500 years ago:

> Most people have too much; I alone seem to be missing something. Mine is indeed the mind of an ignoramus in its unadulterated simplicity. I am but a guest in this world. While others rush about to get things done, I accept what is offered. I alone seem foolish, earning little and spending less (Tao Te Ching, 20thverse). [4]

Lao-tzu discerns that others appear to have abundant things, such as wealth and achievements.

However, he feels that he is lacking in some way. He acknowledges his simple mindset. The philosopher believes he is merely a temporary presence in this world, so he does not feel the need to own or control his surroundings. Lao-tzu notes that while most people are busy striving and rushing to achieve goals, he prefers to accept what comes his way without trying for more. Though his life choices may seem foolish to others, he prefers a minimalist lifestyle and is content with few possessions.

Reflecting on the wisdom propagated by the wise men of ancient times, what gives contentment is being satisfied with our necessities. I am truly happy for those working hard in this world so that they can enjoy the luxuries on offer. And I enjoy viewing some of the most impressive homes on my daily travels through the Lincolnshire countryside. But what I am looking forward to tomorrow is my trip to Waddingham, where the narrow stream courses through the village green. The pavements will be covered in cowslips, dog violets, and snowdrops. The air will be permeated with the smell of lavender as I brush past and the possible smell of freshly cut grass. Walking alongside the bin lorry, I will hear the sounds of blackbirds and robins as they look inquisitively at me and say their morning greeting. I will feel the warm sun on my face and know I am truly free.

Chapter 3

Children love bin lorries.

'Know that success and inner peace are your birthright, that you are a child of God and as such you're entitled to a life filled with joy, love, and happiness',

Wayne Dyer [5]

One thing I never expected when taking this job was seeing the excitement on the faces of young children when the bin lorry goes by. A day seldom goes by when you don't see their faces light up at the sight of our bin lorry. We sometimes see them standing on the path, waving a greeting. They sometimes stand at the front door alongside their mothers. One dad brings his young child to the sitting room window every Friday morning and points us out to him. Without fail, every Friday morning, there are at least three young children who look out for us on Cherry Paddock's estate. Sometimes, I am asked to cover for a colleague on annual leave, taking me to towns I usually don't frequent. Yet, here, too, we will encounter children waving through windows. While working at Bishop Norton the other day, we saw a mother picking blackberries with her three young daughters. They took the time to exchange a friendly greeting with our driver, and the youngest girl gave our driver a small flower she had picked for him to put in the van. I have often marvelled at children's fascination with bin lorries. Adults may hear an irritating noise that wakes them from their peaceful slumber or recoil at the stench of the collected waste on a hot summer day – children react very differently. Why do we lose our innocence as we grow older? Why do we tend to become more opinionated and judgemental of others?

When I think of very young children, I often consider how God gives us, as parents, the most beautiful, perfect gift. However, as parents, teachers, friends, and society, we spend a lifetime trying to control them, influence them into our thinking, and effectively change who they are and are meant to be. It is as if, at birth, we are the very best versions of ourselves, sent here by God as a unique gift to this world. As we grow older, we become moulded by its influential way of thinking and lose sight of our innocence, purity, and spirituality. As a child growing up, my teachers always told me off for talking too much in class. As parents, we tell our children to keep quiet, sit still, not touch anything when visiting others, and listen to what our parents teach us. Although this is what is socially acceptable, is it right? What if our infant children are wise, and we should watch them intently and learn to be more childlike in our everyday lives? The wisest man who lived once said: 'Truly I tell you, unless you change and become like little children, you will never enter the kingdom of heaven' (NIV Bible, Matthew 18:3). [6]

When out on our bin rounds, I cannot help but marvel at the wisdom of very young children. They do not view us carriers as dirty. They do not pull up their noses as we pass by. They do not care what others think when they wave to us. I have grandchildren of a similar age, and they have this innate wisdom that we, as adults, have lost along the way. Infants do not see colour or distinction in nationalities; they do not react differently to one being wealthy or poor; they don't care whether you are wearing an Armani suit or bright orange reflective work clothes; they do not pull away from you if your clothes are a bit dirty from a hard day's work and you emit a distasteful odour. They are our most beautiful gift, as they teach us everything we need to know about unconditional love and acceptance. I am not suggesting that we as adults should not have our favourite friends, those we are particularly drawn to. I suggest that we take off these lenses that the world has given us to wear and start to look at everything from a child's perspective. We should love others unconditionally. Some may rub us up incorrectly, but we must learn to love them for who they are. In addition to this, we should love ourselves for who we are and not try to change. We have all been given as gifts from God to this world, and we should reflect his qualities in our styles. As adults, inadvertently, by our behaviour, we teach children only to love those who conform to our rules. In introspection, when we show our dislike of others or expect them to be who we want them to be, we are saying to God: 'I don't like this one, and I'm going to change them into someone I find more desirable.'

This is a situation that nearly all parents experience daily. In their desire to see their children succeed, many parents impose their dreams and expectations on them. I believe my father is unaware of what I do for a living. He certainly wouldn't be pleased with how I make my living if he knew. I was raised in sunny South Africa, a country with a complex history and deeply ingrained social norms. Growing up, it was unheard of to see white people collecting rubbish. This task was typically assigned to non-white persons, as white individuals viewed such work beneath them. This societal norm was reflected in the aspirations parents held for their children. They often encouraged their children to pursue prestigious careers such as doctors, nurses, lawyers, or successful business people.

Parents' aspirations for their children can sometimes be overwhelming. When children deviate from the path their parents have meticulously planned for them, parents can be quick to express their disappointment. This reaction can stem from a place of love and concern, but it often overlooks the child's dreams and aspirations. Instead of imposing their desires, parents should support their children's unique ambitions and respect their journeys. Allowing children to explore their interests and make mistakes is crucial for their development. Through these experiences, children gain valuable lessons that promote self-awareness and personal growth. Through this exploration and the occasional misstep, they learn resilience and discover their true passions. Supporting children fosters a sense of independence and confidence, helping them become well-rounded individuals capable of forging their paths in life.

As a binman, I understand that I cannot alone navigate life. If my teeth are in bad shape, I need a dentist. When I feel unwell, I rely on a doctor or nurse. When it comes to investing the extra money from my pay cheque (since I get paid way too much), I seek advice from my accountant. In society, we all rely on each other to function smoothly. Without this interdependence, society would fall apart. While parents naturally want the best for their children, it is crucial to recognize that each child's path is unique. By respecting and supporting their children's dreams, parents can help them grow into their true selves, equipped with the skills and experiences necessary to navigate life's complexities. And who knows, if we are not too judgmental of the aspirations of our young ones, we might have enough binmen in future generations.

Chapter 4

Discovering wisdom from the depths of black bins.

'Food waste is like stealing from the table of those who are poor and hungry'.

Pope Francis [7]

It is common knowledge among binmen that black bin week is our least favourite week. We know that those bins are going to break our backs. No matter the village, hamlet, or housing estate we find ourselves in, we have a challenging task ahead of us to get the job done. You might not be aware, but there is no time for breaks on black bin week, as it is a fight to get the job done before the incinerator closes at Lincoln. And then you come across houses where three black bins aren't sufficient, as they also have a few extra bags of side waste that need to be disposed of. At times like this, I reflect on my black bin at home, collected fortnightly on

Mondays. I find myself asking: How full is my bin? What am I discarding? How much am I wasting?

When people do not know how to recycle their waste, they throw everything into a black bin to avoid confusion. You would think this is why the black bins are so heavy, but it is not. Most seasoned binmen will tell you that the biggest culprit is food waste. And I am not just talking about some food scraped off the plate. I'm referring to the shocking amount of food being thrown away that could feed others. I have lost count of the times I have seen sealed packets of bacon, tins of food, bottles of juice and milk, and even whole large wheels of cheese fall out of the bins into the back of the lorry. Yes, you heard right. It was not your ordinary piece of cheese bought from Tesco, but large cheese wheels.

It Is difficult for me to read the news about pensioners all around the country struggling to get by and visiting food banks to ensure they get enough to eat for the day. There are children all around Britain whose school dinner might be the only meal they get for the day. Thousands of people were risking their lives and limbs to cross the channel to get to England for a better life, who did not even have one meal a day. So, when I see the amount of food waste every fortnight, it stirs strong emotions inside of me. I will never forget something that happened to me during my primary school years while growing up in South Africa. My mother made us some jam sandwiches for lunch, and I did not really care for the taste and texture of jam, so when my mom was not looking, I opened the lounge window and threw the sandwich outside into the flowerbed. I did not know that my mom would do some gardening that afternoon, but she found that sandwich. My mom, a wonderful woman with solid values, was not pleased with my lack of appreciation. So she called me home from the park across the road and told me I had to eat the sandwich she had found. To add a bit of detail to the story, I must mention that by now, I couldn't see any jam as the sandwich was covered in ants. I can tell you from personal experience those pesky ants can indeed move fast, and when you take your time eating an ant-covered jam sandwich, some will venture up your nose. My advice to anyone having to eat any form of crawling insect is to eat it as quickly as possible. Today's children might view this as abuse or cruelty. But looking back, I have admiration for my mum, who taught me a valuable lesson that day: not to waste food. I can assure you that was the last and only time I wasted food. When I see loads of food drop into the back of the bin lorry, I often think back on that pivotal day.

The difficulty is that we live in a society that teaches us to look the other way when we see the hardships that others are encountering. It is as if we are constantly being trained to look after number one, which is ourselves. People facing hardships in other lands, with no food, are desperate to get here, but we want to send them back to Africa. We are, in effect, saying we don't want to know about your troubles; we don't want to help you; you are someone else's problem; why don't you return to where you came from? What has happened to humanity when we have no concern for the afflicted, only caring about our needs and desires? How can we live in reasonable comfort, with most of our needs taken care of, and when someone cries out for help, we refuse them our help? What is worse is when comedians make a joke about the poor and hungry in other nations of the world. Have we become so insensitive that we find the hunger and suffering of others a joke?

Thomas Hobbes, a renowned English philosopher from the sixteenth and seventeenth centuries, did not blame society for humanity's uncaring attitude; he blamed the individual. Living during the English Civil War, Hobbes was well aware of humanity's capacity for harm. His famous book Leviathan argues that humans have a strong drive to increase their happiness by fulfilling their desires. The problem arises when these desires conflict with others seeking the same things. With resources like food often in short supply, as seen today, Hobbes believed that competition and conflict would naturally follow. Since any person can kill another, take what they want, or protect what they have, violence or the threat of it is ever-present. If every human being had the same amount of food to eat every day as the next, would people be stealing food from shops or risking their lives in rubber dinghies to cross the English Channel?

Some might argue that it's impractical to send a wheel of cheese to countries where people are less fortunate, as the transport costs exceed the value of the cheese. While this is true, it misses the broader issue of food waste. Every time we throw away food, we should remember how many hungry people it could have fed. Food shortages endanger real lives, and we must acknowledge the disparity. I often reflect on how different my life could have been if I had been born into poverty, unable to meet my basic needs. Just because I have been fortunate, does that entitle me to ignore the suffering of others and live in a way that disrespects their existence?

It's striking how people In a secular society often blame God for the world's injustices, hunger, sickness, and suffering. However, examining the situation more closely, I see human greed. People hoard resources they can't consume and then sell them at premium prices instead of sharing them with the less fortunate. In contrast, Jesus spoke of God's generosity, saying, 'Would any of you give your hungry child a stone if the child asked for some bread? Would you give your child a snake if the child asked for a fish? As bad as you are, you still know how to give good gifts to your children. But your heavenly Father is even more ready to give good things to people who ask' (Contemporary English Version, Matthew 7: 9 – 11). [8]

The problem isn't that God is indifferent to human hunger; humans refuse to help those in need. They choose to hoard, store, and sell rather than give freely.

We inadvertently harm ourselves when we resist our natural inclination to help others. We are born with an innate ability to assist others, and we must pay attention to this. Ancient wisdom echoes this, teaching us that true wealth is derived from giving to others. This profound concept is beautifully encapsulated in verse 81 of the Tao Te Ching, which declares, 'The Master has no possessions. The more he does for others, the happier he is. The more he gives to others, the wealthier he is.' [9] This verse suggests that genuine contentment and prosperity are not found in material possessions but in selfless acts of giving and helping others.

The notion that accumulating material wealth and possessions can often lead to a sense of emptiness and dissatisfaction is not a new one. However, when we redirect our focus towards the well-being of others and actively contribute to their happiness and prosperity, we tap into a more profound sense of fulfilment and joy. This generous approach to life enriches our existence in ways that material wealth cannot. Moreover, it underscores the interconnectedness of humanity. We foster a more harmonious and compassionate society by sharing our resources and aiding those in need. This sense of community and mutual support is a source of true wealth, nurturing relationships and creating a network of care and generosity that benefits everyone. The wisdom of the Tao Te Ching urges us to shift our focus from self-centred accumulation to outward generosity. It teaches us that giving freely and helping others unlocks a more prosperous, more meaningful life.

I eagerly anticipate the day when the bins on my black bin collection route are noticeably lighter. This change would be a clear sign that my neighbours are becoming less wasteful and more mindful of their consumption habits' impact on the world around them. This shift would indicate a heightened environmental awareness and a more profound sense of empathy and consideration for their fellow human beings, especially those struggling with hunger and poverty. By being more prudent with their resources, my neighbours would demonstrate an understanding that excess and waste are ethically and socially irresponsible when so many people are in need. It would mean that they are taking steps to ensure that the resources they once wasted are now better utilized, possibly even redistributed to help those less fortunate. Knowing that this transformation in waste habits reflects my neighbours' pursuit of a more meaningful and fulfilling life would bring me great joy. It would suggest that they are moving beyond a lifestyle of convenience and excess toward one that values sustainability, community, and social responsibility. Witnessing my community embrace these values would be incredibly heartening. The lighter bins symbolize a collective commitment to living more thoughtfully and compassionately, ultimately contributing to a more just and equitable world. This evolution would enhance our neighbourhood and serve as a beacon of hope and inspiration for broader societal change.

Chapter 5

Encountering generosity in a self-centred society.

'You have not lived today until you have done something for someone who can never repay you'.

John Bunyan [10]

Today, I got to cover for a carrier who had the day off. But this was alright, as I got to work in Welton. Welton can mean different things to different people. It is the quintessential village, a reminder to me of what I love so much about England. It is also home to William Farr Comprehensive Secondary School, which has a good reputation. However, when I think of Welton, the word 'generosity' comes to mind. The Cambridge dictionary defines generous as follows: 'willing to give money, help, kindness, etc., especially more than is usual or expected'.

When we look at the world around us, "generous" isn't the first thing that comes to mind. Society is becoming increasingly self-centred, with people focusing more on themselves and less on others. The rise of social media has only exacerbated this issue. These platforms encourage users to focus on their lives, constantly sharing updates about their achievements and opinions. This obsession with likes and followers can easily lead to narcissism, creating a competitive environment where people measure their worth against the popularity of others. Depending on their social media status, individuals might develop an inflated sense of self or feelings of inadequacy. As people become trapped in this cycle of seeking constant validation, they lose authenticity in their quest for perfection or approval. This environment does not foster wholesome, meaningful, and valuable relationships.

Of all the rounds I have worked on, Welton is the one that truly stands out. I wonder if this is because it has more older residents than other villages where I have worked. It's well known that older individuals tend to rely less on social media, valuing close personal relationships far more than the superficial connections often promoted online. These individuals don't need the internet or the opinions of others to guide their decisions. When they express a preference, it's their own, not the crowd's influence. They trust their instincts and know their minds, remaining unaffected by the sway of popular opinion.

Therefore, showing kindness and generosity or offering a friendly greeting should come from the heart, not as a bid for public recognition or likes. Online posts flaunting acts of kindness are offensive. I feel sympathy for the recipients of these acts when the benefactors boast about their good deeds. I once spoke with a man in Sheffield who shared that he disliked going to a particular soup kitchen because the local priest would always start by boasting about the church's charitable deeds. This made him feel used. Why is it so difficult for people to show kindness without expecting anything? Why must there always be an ulterior motive? One of my favourite Bible verses is when Jesus says, 'So when you give to the poor, do not sound a trumpet before you, as the hypocrites do in the synagogues and on the streets so that people will praise them. Truly, I say to you that they have their reward in full. But when you give to the poor, do not let your left hand know what your right hand is doing so that your charitable giving will be in secret (NASB Bible, Matthew 6: 2 – 4). [11] Would you not agree that these are graceful sentiments?

Throughout all my regular rounds, I have had the heartwarming experience of being offered cold drinks, chocolates, biscuits, and even slices of cake by thoughtful customers. These gestures have left a lasting impression on me, as they exemplify genuine acts of kindness. Despite my inability to do anything in return, some customers take the time to extend their generosity unexpectedly. These meaningful encounters are a poignant reminder of the goodwill and compassion that still thrive within our communities. One hot summer day, a customer in Market Rasen handed us ice-cold drinks as we passed her house, her smile refreshing as the drink itself. Another time, during the festive season, an elderly gentleman at Waddingham gave us a box of cakes, explaining that his wife had baked extra just for the binmen. These experiences bring to mind the analogy of being openhanded, vividly conveying generosity and receptiveness. I always picture an extended open hand, palm facing upwards. This image starkly contrasts with that of a closed fist. When the hand is clenched into a fist, it becomes impossible to share anything with others; holding on tightly precludes any form of giving. In contrast, an open hand symbolizes the willingness to give freely, unreservedly offering what one has to those in need.

Furthermore, this analogy extends beyond the act of giving. It is also crucial to recognize that a closed fist prevents the act of giving and inhibits receiving. When the hand is tightly shut, it cannot accept any offerings from others. Conversely, an open hand, poised to give, is simultaneously ready to receive. This duality emphasizes that generosity is a two-way street. By keeping our hands open, we remain receptive to the gifts and support that others may offer, fostering a continuous cycle of giving and receiving that enriches both the giver and the receiver.

These moments made me feel appreciated and reinforced the sense of community and mutual respect that often gets overlooked in our fast-paced lives. After savouring a tasty treat, we understand that we need extra effort, as a moment on the lips is a lifetime on the hips. It's a small price to pay for the joy of experiencing such kindness. These small yet significant acts of generosity remind me daily of the goodness in people and inspire me to approach my work with even more dedication and a positive spirit.

I also enjoy working in Welton because I can interact with the many elderly couples and individuals who come out for a brief chat. This simple interaction has become one of the highlights of my rounds. While some binmen see their job as merely moving from one bin to the next, a good binman understands the importance of connecting with the public. We are providing a public service, and what value does that service have if we cannot even offer a friendly greeting?

Many of our elderly residents lead very isolated lives, and they look forward to seeing a friendly face or receiving a warm greeting each week. For some, we might be the only person they see all week. I often think about a sweet elderly lady who waits by her gate with a cheerful wave and kind words. Her stories about her late husband and her garden brighten our day as much as if not more than, our presence brightens hers. A retired gentleman also shares a different joke with us every week. We often walk away, chuckling out loud, with a spring in our steps. Our brief conversations remind me of the importance of staying connected with others, no matter how short the interaction. While we may not always have the time to sit down for a cup of coffee and a slice of cake, there is always time for a brief hello. These moments of connection, though fleeting, are precious. They remind me that our work goes beyond the physical task of collecting waste; it also involves building a sense of community and showing that we care.

Our connection with the older residents of Welton is genuinely heartwarming and makes my work there incredibly fulfilling. It's a privilege to bring joy and companionship to those who might otherwise feel isolated. Their smiles, stories, and gratitude make every day on the job worthwhile, constantly reminding me of the profound impact a simple, friendly interaction can have on someone's life. Please take a moment the next time your binmen are in your area to step outside and greet them. A simple "hello" or a friendly wave can make a significant difference. This small act of acknowledgment and kindness not only brightens their day but also positively impacts their mood.

Engaging with others, even briefly, can lead to feelings of happiness and satisfaction. Smiling and connecting with someone in your community fosters a sense of belonging and mutual respect. So, don't hesitate to extend a friendly gesture – you may be pleasantly surprised at how much joy it can bring to you and the person you greet.

Chapter 6

Indra's Net.

'The biggest thing I've learned is that it's not about me. All of the things that I do have to be about bringing service to the world and helping people shift their perceptions'.

Gabrielle Bernstein [12]

The Flower Garland Sutra, an ancient Buddhist text, vividly describes the heavenly realm of Indra, the king of the gods, where an exquisite net woven by a master artisan is suspended. This extraordinary net stretches infinitely in all directions and is adorned with countless glistening, multifaceted jewels. Each jewel reflects every other jewel in the net, creating a mesmerizing, endless display of interconnected reflections. When closely examining any individual jewel, one can see that it reflects all the other jewels, each of which also reflects all the others, creating an infinitely intricate and beautiful cascade of reflections.

The first time I heard of this ancient tale, it had a lasting impact on my understanding of the world and the part I play within society. Growing up, I had a connection with my immediate family members, children in my class at school, and neighbours that I came into contact with. But that was as far as it went. There was no internet and no social media. My connection and influence were minimal. If I had not read the weekly Sunday Times, I would have had no idea what was happening worldwide. Even then, the news I was reading was already a few days old. When we get to South Kelsey every Tuesday morning, I often notice the secondary school children walking to the nearby bus stop on their way to school. Most of the time, they do not even look up when I greet them, as they are so engrossed in their mobile phones. I am lucky to receive any form of recognition. Considering the World Wide Web and the ability to readily share so much information at the tap of a button, what intrigues me is that society is becoming more polarised. The internet and social media have become conduits pushing people further apart.

Instead of promoting unity and oneness, we must differentiate ourselves and stand out. I firmly believe in being true to oneself, but when this independence fosters extreme diversity, it creates a problem. When I observe nature and see a dog walking with its owner, perhaps with only three legs, I still recognize it as a dog. And undoubtedly, that dog prefers to be identified as such. If society asked this poor animal to question its identity, why can't you be a fish and swim? Why can't you be a bird and fly? Such confusion would be unfair to the animal. Yet, this is what our world is doing. The pronouns people use to identify themselves are increasing daily. One day, I might identify as a Jedi master, and the next, as a woodland fairy. The issue with this fluidity is that I lose connection with others who struggle to understand me as my identity shifts.

Returning to the tale of Indra's Net, we learn that each jewel reflects all the others, illustrating that every part of the universe contains the essence of the whole. We may be individual 'jewels,' but what we are and who we are contains the essence of all humanity. This aligns with the Buddhist teaching that all things are interwoven and that understanding any single part can provide insight into the nature of the cosmos.

I have come to a deep realization that our interconnectedness brings a profound sense of responsibility for each of us. This interconnectedness means that our positive or negative actions have far-reaching impacts on the world around us. Therefore, we must demonstrate empathy and compassion in our daily interactions. When we show compassion to those in need, we do more than offer help; we contribute to brightening their light. This act of kindness creates a ripple effect, reflecting on us and enhancing our well-being. Conversely, when we are cruel or unkind, we diminish their light; in doing so, we also diminish the light that could have been reflected back to us. Our actions, whether good or bad, influence the entire net of life, and in turn, this net influences us.

Understanding this interconnectedness leads to a profound ethical awareness: harming others ultimately means hurting ourselves. This realization should heighten our concern for how we treat our environment, our fellow human beings, and all living creatures. It becomes imperative to avoid thoughtless actions and instead cultivate mindfulness in our daily behaviours. Every act carries weight; a careless deed can have severe implications as it ripples through the interconnected net of existence. Consider the analogy of an unattended campfire: what starts as a small, manageable flame can quickly escalate into a devastating wildfire, destroying entire woodlands.

Similarly, when we are careless and neglect our responsibility to care for the environment, we set in motion events that could lead to the degradation and eventual destruction of the environment we rely on for survival. Therefore, we must approach our daily actions with a heightened sense of mindfulness and responsibility. Doing so ensures that our actions contribute positively to the net of life, fostering a world where empathy, compassion, and care are paramount. This mindful approach benefits those around us and ensures the sustainability and health of the interconnected world we all share.

Understanding how we relate to others leads us to a deeper spiritual awareness of our place in the world. The world does not exist to cater to our every need; instead, we are here to serve one another. While it is easy to become absorbed in our ambitions, desires, and challenges, true fulfillment arises from looking beyond ourselves and considering our broader impact on the world. When we focus solely on ourselves, our perspective becomes limited, and our actions are often driven by self-interest. This can create a cycle of relentless pursuit for personal gain, which may provide temporary satisfaction but usually leaves a more profound sense of purpose unfulfilled. However, when we shift our focus to serving others, we tap into a more significant source of meaning and satisfaction. By turning our attention outward and prioritizing the well-being of others, we not only enrich their lives but also bring more profound meaning and joy to our own. Ensuring that we act positively towards those around us creates a ripple effect, spreading positivity and beneficially influencing the world. This outward focus fosters a sense of interconnectedness and shared purpose, leading to a more fulfilling and harmonious existence.

Chapter 7

The Duality of Existence: Creation's Two Faces.

'What is life without loss, love without loneliness, ecstasy without pain? You can't have one without the other or you could never appreciate either'.

Courtney M. Privett [13]

Reflecting on the past few months of working as a binman, I am grappling with a persistent challenge – extensive roadkill. Initially, I had hoped that frequent exposure to these distressing scenes would diminish their impact on me. Still, I have come to realize that the emotional toll remains significant. Each time our route takes us down the A15, and I come across a lifeless badger on the roadside, I am flooded with a deep sense of grief. Despite not being directly involved in its demise, I am compelled to express sincere remorse for the loss of life. I fervently wish that the animal did not suffer unduly and that its passing was swift and merciful. These encounters often lead me to ponder the reasons behind the tragic fate that befell this innocent creature. The repetitive nature of these encounters brings a mix of sorrow and reflection. Every animal I see serves as a reminder of life's fragility and the often harsh realities wildlife face in urban environments. The sight of a lifeless creature, once full of life and potential, now lying motionless on the road stirs a profound sadness within me.

Later in our shift, we leave Bishop Norton and drive past a few detached homes on the village outskirts. Every time, without fail, we hear the barking of a shih tzu as soon as the bin lorry engine is within earshot. He lives with a kind older lady who lets him run out to greet us at the gate, eagerly waiting for his treat. His excitement when he sees us is boundless; he dashes around the large garden with limitless energy. He embodies vitality and joy. A few minutes later, as we move on to the next house, my colleagues and I can't help but smile broadly. In moments like these, I often wonder if we appreciate the happy times more deeply because we've known pain. With his unbridled enthusiasm and zest for life, this cheerful little dog starkly contrasts the sad scenes of roadkill I encounter. His pure, innocent joy is a powerful reminder of the beauty and vitality of life, a reminder that is especially poignant after the sadness of witnessing death.

On the same day, I experience the duality of existence, witnessing both life and death. This juxtaposition has made me more acutely aware of the transient nature of life and the importance of cherishing every moment. The Shih Tzu's vitality and the melancholy sight of roadkill together form a tapestry of experiences that shape my understanding of life's impermanence. These experiences have deepened my empathy and have made me more reflective about the interconnectedness of all living beings. Through the highs and lows, I am reminded of the resilience of life and the inevitable presence of joy and sorrow.

The concept of duality is evident in the cyclical rhythm of life, mainly when we observe the behaviour of plants and trees. Consider a lavish and fragrant lavender bush, which blooms with beautiful purple flowers and emits a delightful aroma during the summer months, showcasing the vibrancy of life. However, as the seasons transition, the lavender bush sheds its flowers. It begins to wither, symbolizing the process of decay and death. While it may be disheartening to witness the loss of these beautiful blooms, we can take solace in knowing that this transitional phase is not permanent. The lavender bush will once again spring to life in the following months, illustrating the innate duality of death and renewal essential to plants' natural world. This cycle perpetuates the continuity and rejuvenation of life in the plant kingdom.

As I observe the transformation of the lavender bush, I profoundly reflect on the implications of this natural cycle on my existence. The question arises: When I depart from this world, is that truly the end? But then I consider why our Creator has bestowed these remarkable demonstrations of transition—from life to death and back to life. Our Heavenly Father could have designed plants to bloom perpetually without the necessity of withering and renewing. Yet, He chose to create a world where life is marked by cycles of decay and rebirth. This intentional design leads me to believe that these natural lessons are profound reminders that our current life is not the entirety of our existence.

When a plant begins to wither, it is tempting to see this as the end of its journey. It has lived its life and seemingly completed its purpose. However, it tells a different story when it springs back to life. Unlike plants, we humans possess the ability to think deeply, to question, and to seek meaning. This capacity drives us to ponder whether our brief earthly life is all there is. The wise King Solomon once said, "God has set eternity in the human heart" (Ecclesiastes 3:11, NIV). [14] This profound statement suggests that within us lies an inherent sense of eternity, an understanding that there is more to life than what we can perceive and experience in our current existence.

The cycles of nature, particularly the life cycle of a plant, are crafted with intention. They remind us of the transient nature of our earthly lives and hint at the existence of something beyond. As the lavender bush dies and flourishes, it serves as a metaphor for our lives and the possibility of life beyond death. This natural process encourages us to look beyond the immediate, to trust that there is a greater purpose and a continuation beyond what we can see. Through these lessons in nature, it becomes clear that our lives are part of a much grander design that encompasses eternity and offers hope beyond our mortal experiences.

Every day, I encounter a world filled with duality and contrasts, and I cannot help but believe that these experiences are here to teach me something profound. This interplay of opposites seems essential for my understanding and appreciation of life. For instance, could I genuinely relish summer's long, warm days without first enduring the short, cold, and dark days of winter? The beauty and vitality of a sunny day become much more pronounced after experiencing the stillness and detachment of a night's sleep. The delight in savouring the creamy richness of a cheesecake is heightened by contrasting it with the often-divisive taste of Brussels sprouts.

These differences and opposites help me to comprehend and cherish the various states of existence more deeply. It is through the experience of these contrasts that my life becomes uniquely rich and instructive. Each opposite not only highlights its counterpart but also allows me to appreciate the inherent qualities of both. The dualities I face daily - from joy and sorrow to comfort and discomfort - play a crucial role in my personal growth. By navigating through these contrasting experiences, I develop a more profound understanding of the world and a deeper appreciation for the nuances of my life. I find the essence of my existence within this dance of opposites. The challenges, comforts, pleasures, and pains all contribute to a more comprehensive and enriched understanding of what it means to live.

Thus, these daily encounters with duality are not mere coincidences but are fundamental elements of my journey. They are here to guide me and teach me resilience, gratitude, and perspective. Each contrast I experience helps me to grow, not just in understanding the world around me but also in appreciating the intricate balance that defines my life. This balance, this dynamic interplay of opposites, ultimately shapes my character and my appreciation for the life I am given.

When I delve deeper into these reflections, it leads me to reconsider the very essence of life. Questions arise, such as: Why am I here in the first place? Why do I experience the life I have been given rather than someone else's experience? As I ponder these profound questions, I sense that my life, with all its rich and varied experiences, has been granted to me for a specific reason. The dualities I encounter - joy and sorrow, light and darkness, pleasure and pain - provide a delicate balance that fosters understanding, growth, and meaning. These contrasts are not just random occurrences but integral to my existence. They shape my perspective and contribute to my personal development. These experiences are necessary for my life to have the depth and complexity that make it uniquely mine. Each experience, whether positive or negative, plays a crucial role in my journey. The challenges teach me resilience and strength, while the moments of joy and beauty remind me of the goodness that exists in the world. This interplay of opposites enriches my understanding of life and allows me to appreciate its multifaceted nature.

These lessons and experiences are not just for this life but are also preparing me for something beyond. The growth and wisdom I gain here might be essential for a life hereafter, one that I will appreciate even more because of what I have learned in this world. The notion that my current life is a preparation for a future existence gives profound significance to every moment I experience. In this light, my life is a continuous process of learning and evolving. The dualities I face are teachers guiding me towards a deeper understanding of myself and the world around me. They help me to recognize the transient nature of my current existence and to grasp the possibility of something greater beyond this life. Thus, when I philosophize about the meaning of life, I conclude that every experience, every contrast, and every lesson is part of a grander design. This design is meant to prepare me for life hereafter, enriching my soul and preparing me to appreciate the eternal with a wisdom that can only be gained through living the full spectrum of human experience.

Chapter 8

Keep your phone switched on.

'In Life, every gain has a corresponding loss
& every loss has a
corresponding gain'.
Yadu [15]

One of the challenges I still need help with as an agency binman is the uncertainty of my work schedule. Since I'm not part of a regular team, I only get called in to fill shifts as needed. This means I'm constantly on standby, waiting for an opportunity to work. The agency requires me always to keep my phone on in case someone else can't make it to work. If I get called, I must drop everything and get to work as quickly as possible. As I get older, this situation is becoming increasingly difficult for me. The constant uncertainty makes sleeping hard, as I never know whether I'll be called to work. I had the chance to reflect on this obstacle today while looking out at the cow paddock overlooking St. Georges Lane in Lincoln. As I waited for the lorry to pull alongside, I watched the cows grazing peacefully in the adjacent fields. They appeared content, starkly contrasting my uncertain work schedule. These cows likely know where they will be daily with some certainty. Although I'm not a farmer and can't say how cows are kept, I imagine they are confident they will be fed daily. It seems unlikely that a farmer would feed them one day and then neglect to feed them the next.

Furthermore, I can't picture a scenario where a cow has to be on standby, waiting for another cow to skip a meal so it can take its place in the meadow. The cows seemed so carefree, trusting that their farmer had their welfare in mind. This realization highlighted the contrast between their predictable routine and my unpredictable work life. As I watched them graze, I couldn't help but envy their sense of security and trust in their caregiver. It made me long for a similar sense of stability and assurance in my life, free from the constant uncertainty and anxiety of waiting for the next call to work.

As humans, our lives are incredibly complicated. If you speak to anyone who has lived a whole life, they will likely tell you that nothing in life is straightforward. Reflecting on this complexity, I realize that my need for more work often comes at a cost to others. For me to get an extra shift, someone else must fail to show up for theirs. This means that someone else must lose what was originally theirs for me to gain. This situation creates a moral dilemma that extends beyond the uncertainty of my work schedule. It's not just about the anxiety of waiting for the next call; it's about the uncomfortable reality that my opportunities come from someone else's misfortune. This notion doesn't sit well with me, as I have never wanted to benefit at the expense of others.

Philosophizing the matter further, it becomes clear how interconnected our lives are and how our gains and losses are often linked to those of others. The idea that I depend on someone else's failure for my success creates a deep sense of unease. It feels wrong to hope that something terrible will happen to someone else so that I can have work. This moral conflict adds another layer of difficulty to an already challenging situation, making me question the fairness and ethics of my circumstances. Ultimately, this reflection highlights a broader truth about human existence: our lives are filled with complex, often uncomfortable trade-offs that force us to confront difficult ethical questions. In my case, the need for work and the desire to maintain my integrity are in constant tension, adding to the overall sense of complication and struggle in my life.

This also reminds me of the challenges I encountered while studying at university. Travelling weekly from West Yorkshire to Lincoln was incredibly difficult. My wife and I spent more than a year finding accommodation in Lincoln. A single student can always find shared accommodation with other students. Still, things get more complicated when you are married and have an adorable Yorkshire Terrier—finding a suitable home that accommodates our unique needs proved arduous. We finally managed to secure our new home in Lincolnshire, for which we were extremely grateful. However, this achievement came at a significant cost. At the time, we couldn't understand why it was so difficult to find the right place. We had gone through countless listings, endured numerous rejections, and faced uncertainty about where we would live. Weeks after we moved in, our new neighbours told us about the previous tenant, who had recently passed away. This revelation casts a shadow over our relief and gratitude. Reflecting on this, I felt a deep sense of sorrow. I realized that our gain—a stable and comfortable home—came from someone else's loss. The thought weighed heavily on me. I would have preferred to continue the exhausting journey from West Yorkshire to Lincoln if it meant the previous tenants could have had more time with their family and loved ones. The comfort and stability we found were bittersweet, tainted by the knowledge that it was made possible by another's tragedy. This experience underscored the interconnectedness of our lives and the often-unseen costs of our successes. It reminded me that our triumphs can sometimes be linked to the misfortunes of others. This reality complicates our sense of achievement and gratitude.

In reflecting on these experiences, I am reminded of the delicate balance between our desires and the impacts they can have on others. Whether needing work shifts that depend on others' absences or finding a home that became available due to someone's passing, these situations highlight our lives' complexities and moral nuances. They teach us empathy and the importance of considering the broader implications of our actions and circumstances.

When we pray for our needs and desires, we often focus on our perspective, sense of need, and sense of urgency. However, it's important to remember that God's perspective encompasses the needs and desires of all people. Each prayer is a plea from one of His children, and each child is equally valued and loved. This means that when we ask for something, we are not just placing our hopes and wishes before God but also unintentionally setting up a scenario where fulfilling our prayer could mean another's goes unanswered. Consider the complexity of the situation from God's viewpoint. He looks down and sees all His children, each with hopes, dreams, and requests. Fulfilling one prayer might mean disappointing another. Someone might pray for rain to nourish their crops, while another prays for sunny weather at Skegness. These conflicting desires place God in a position where He must balance the scales of countless prayers, all equally earnest and heartfelt. This dynamic illustrates the profound interconnectedness of our lives and the potential costs involved in answered prayers. When we pray for success, healing, or blessings, we often do so without fully realizing that these outcomes may require significant shifts in the lives of others. In His infinite wisdom, God must weigh these requests, considering the immediate impact and the broader, long-term consequences for all involved.

In contemplating this, I imagine God experiencing deep compassion and perhaps even sorrow as He navigates these decisions. He sees the bigger picture, understanding the ripple effects of granting or withholding a particular blessing. He must think, "These are both my children; whose wish do I fulfil?" This thought process underscores the complexity and difficulty of divine decision-making. It highlights the intricate balance God must maintain in ensuring fairness and compassion in His responses to our prayers.

Moreover, this reflection invites us to approach prayer with greater humility and awareness. It encourages us to consider not just our own needs but also the potential impact on others. It reminds us to trust in God's wisdom and timing, recognizing that His understanding of our lives and the interconnected nature of all things surpasses our own.

Ultimately, this perspective fosters a more profound sense of empathy and interconnectedness. It calls us to be mindful of the broader implications of our desires and to cultivate a spirit of gratitude for the blessings we receive, knowing that they are part of a larger, divine plan that seeks to balance all His children's needs.

Chapter 9

Mindful Driving: Appreciating Our Furry and Feathered Companions.

'He who is cruel to animals becomes hard also in his dealings with men. We can judge the heart of a man by his treatment of animals'.

Emmanuel Kant [16]

We were finishing off our shift on a farm outside of Burton today. Upon approaching the trade bins, I was drawn to an elderly gentleman conversing with one of the farm workers. What caught my eye was the gentle way he cradled something in his hands. It turned out to be a great spotted woodpecker, which had tragically collided with a glass door or window. The delicate bird appeared fragile, its lifeless body limp in his grasp. What struck me most was his profound reverence for handling the deceased bird. He held it like a priceless treasure despite its life having passed. In his eyes, I glimpsed a sorrow that seemed to echo the loss keenly. This encounter left a deep impression on me, stirring a sense of poignant reflection.

Every day during our work travels, it is impossible not to encounter the unfortunate sight of deceased badgers, foxes, pheasants, deer, rabbits, squirrels, or various bird species along the roadside. What truly pains me is witnessing the remains of an animal repeatedly run over by passing motorists, as if its life held no significance. I vividly remember a recent journey to the Lake District when a speeding car zoomed past us, and a small rabbit darted onto the road. Fear etched across its face; it hesitated, uncertain of its next move. What stung the most was the driver's utter disregard; they didn't even tap their brakes, sealing the rabbit's fate in an instant. They collided with it and raced on, indifferent to the life extinguished. Beside me, my wife was overcome with anguish, her cry echoing the injustice of a life snuffed out as inconsequential. At that moment, the contrasting responses to the loss of life became starkly evident among the occupants of the other vehicle and my wife. For one, the sight of the rabbit's life abruptly ending stirred a profound sense of loss and sorrow. This individual recognized the intrinsic value of the creature's existence and felt a genuine pang of grief at its untimely demise. Conversely, to the other vehicle's driver, the incident passed unnoticed, perhaps lost in the rush of daily life or lacking the empathetic connection to register the event's significance fully. In this fleeting moment on the road, perspectives diverged sharply, revealing the spectrum of human attitudes towards the sanctity of life.

I'm incredibly fortunate to have a driver for our bin lorry who prioritizes safety on the road. I've observed his careful approach, particularly when encountering wildlife, where he consistently slows down or brakes. One day, I asked him why he was so considerate, and his response caught me off guard: "I see each animal as if it were a child darting into the road." He didn't delve further into his explanation. However, his compassion for wildlife only complicates his job amidst busy days without breaks and the pressure to meet deadlines. Some might argue that it would be simpler to speed along, disregarding the loss of animal life, given the urgency of our tasks within strict time limits. Moreover, late bin collections sometimes prompt complaints from residents. Despite these challenges, our bin lorry driver has earned my respect and friendship through his conscientious actions.

The eighteenth-century German philosopher Immanuel Kant recognized the sanctity of life. He further asserted that how we treat animals reflects how we will treat fellow humans. Although there were no vehicles in his time, and life moved slower, he would have observed how people treated animals daily. We must ask why people feel entitled to take the lives of animals. What has led us to believe that non-human lives are less significant or valuable than ours?

We explored this topic in one of our Theology classes at university. According to the biblical creation account, God first created fish, then birds, and then land animals, with humans created last. Genesis states, "Then God said, 'Let us make mankind in our image, in our likeness, so that they may rule over the fish in the sea and the birds in the sky, over the livestock and all the wild animals, and over all the creatures that move along the ground'" (NIV Bible, Genesis 1:26). [17]

Could humans believe this authority grants them the right to treat other creatures however they wish? Do God's words endorse our doing as we please with these life forms? Do they imply a hierarchy where we are superior, and animals exist solely to serve our needs? I would argue that the emphasis on being made in the image of God is more significant, as it implies a responsibility to reflect God's nature.

Our understanding of God profoundly shapes how we fulfil our responsibility to care for creation. The ancient Greeks and Romans worshipped a pantheon of gods, many of whom were characterized by warlike and violent behaviour. If we were to model our actions after these deities, we might feel justified in recklessly harming and destroying as we see fit. It's intriguing to observe that, even today, parents sometimes name their children after these mythological figures, for instance, the Norse god Loki, known for his malicious and mischievous nature. In contrast, the God we believe in is fundamentally different. Jesus highlighted our Father's care and compassion, even for the smallest creatures. He said, "Look at the birds in the sky! They don't plant or harvest. They don't even store grain in barns. Yet your Father in heaven takes care of them" (Contemporary English Version, Matthew 6:26). [18] Additionally, He remarked, "Are not two sparrows sold for a small coin? Yet not one of them falls to the ground without your Father's knowledge" (New American Bible,

Matthew 10:29). [19] These teachings underscore a divine attentiveness and concern for all life, which we are called to emulate. Unlike the capricious gods of ancient mythologies, our God exemplifies a nurturing and protective nature. This understanding should guide us to act with compassion and responsibility, ensuring that our treatment of other life forms reflects the same care and respect that God shows for His creation.

These words embody a profound sense of care and awareness. As beings created in the image of God, who provides for all his creatures, we are called to extend that care to all life forms. This responsibility is not about exercising rulership but rather embracing a role of guardianship. Our creator has given us the unique privilege of being protective stewards of all creation. Furthermore, if God knows every animal that dies, he must also understand the circumstances surrounding each death. He will know if an animal was hunted merely for sport, if its life was taken recklessly, or if it was taken out of necessity for food. This divine awareness implies a profound moral responsibility to ensure our actions toward animals are just and considerate. As guardians, we must be mindful of the ethical implications of our behaviour, recognizing that each life is significant and valued by our creator.

Chapter 10

Cheers to Recycling: Exploring the Relationship Between Alcohol and Blue Bins.

'There have been two great narcotics in European civilisation: Christianity and alcohol'.

Friedrich Nietzsche [20]

I used to mistakenly believe that working-class people - those with jobs, homes, and cars - were supposed to be content. However, working in the poorer suburbs has given me the impression that these individuals often lack something. When I visit large homes, I assume the residents have more than enough, perhaps everything they need. So, I thought the working class must have found the perfect balance. I was very wrong. If I were blindfolded and asked to identify which of three blue bins filled with empty glass bottles belonged to the poor, middle class, or wealthy based on the weight of their contents, I would have guessed incorrectly. You might be surprised, or maybe not, to learn that no matter where we work, the entire blue bins tell the same story: the working middle class need a coping mechanism more than the other classes.

In our modern society, we are constantly inundated with false narratives that obscure the actual state of the world. Instead of highlighting important issues, the media often focuses on the extravagant lives of celebrities, promoting an agenda that downplays the harsh realities around us. Social media feeds are filled with people showcasing their seemingly perfect lives. However, the truth is revealed in the small details—like the monthly collection of a blue bin overflowing with wine and alcohol bottles- a stark reminder that life is not always as picturesque as it appears.

When writing this book, the West Lindsey District Council and the government have been at loggerheads over the future of the airbase at Scampton. The council desires to develop the site into a heritage centre, preserving its historical significance and potentially boosting local tourism. On the other hand, the government has proposed using the base to rehome thousands of refugees, addressing the urgent need for housing and support for these individuals. I do not bring this up to delve into the political debates about what is right or wrong. Instead, I want to highlight the broader issue of the thousands upon thousands of desperate individuals who will go to great lengths to reach our shores. Their journeys are dangerous; driven by dire circumstances, I can hardly imagine. While I do not claim to understand the horrors they are fleeing fully, I have some insight into what they hope to find upon arrival. In our society, we often take the material comforts we possess for granted: homes, cars, and jobs. Yet, despite these apparent markers of success, many people in our community struggle with profound unhappiness. The widespread use of alcohol as a socially acceptable means to numb emotional pain is a glaring indicator that something is amiss in our lives.

I often wonder what the refugees would think if, a year from now, they had everything they ever aspired to achieve here. Would they find true contentment, or would they, too, turn to alcohol to cope with their disillusionment? This thought troubles me, as it suggests that our society, despite its wealth and opportunities, may be lacking in genuine fulfilment and well-being. The plight of the refugees seeking a better life highlights a paradox within our society. While we offer safety and opportunities, we also present a lifestyle where material success does not necessarily equate to happiness. This realization calls for a deeper reflection on what it means to live a fulfilling life and how we can create a society that offers refuge and true well-being for all its members.

It is interesting to note that the German philosopher Friedrich Nietzsche also considered Christianity to be a form of narcotic. Nietzsche observed how

Christianity provided explanations for suffering and promised eternal life, serving as a solace for millions. The belief in a higher purpose, divine justice, and the hope of heaven helped individuals endure hardships and tragedies. This spiritual comfort acted as a powerful narcotic, easing the pain of existence and offering hope for a better future. Nietzsche argued that this reliance on Christianity was akin to taking a drug, as it allowed people to bury their heads in the sand and avoid confronting life soberly. He believed that by leaning on the comforting narratives of religion, individuals were essentially blinding themselves to the harsh realities of the world. This, he suggested, was not fundamentally different from using a physical narcotic to escape reality. Both forms of escape prevented people from addressing and understanding the true nature of their existence.

Moreover, this critique extends beyond European societies to include many African refugees who, despite their dire circumstances, often possess a strong faith. These refugees look to a future where God will right this world's wrongs, bring justice, and provide equality for everyone. While their faith offers them hope and comfort, it can also be seen as a way to avoid facing the stark truths of their current situation. Religion, in this sense, acts as their chosen drug, providing an escape from the harshness of their reality.

The irony becomes even more poignant when considering that these refugees might escape a life where religion was their primary means of coping, only to encounter a new life in which they might turn to alcohol as a different form of narcotic. Religious faith often provided a vital source of strength and solace amidst adversity in their previous lives. Their belief systems offered hope, structure, and a sense of community, essential for enduring the hardships they faced daily. Religion served as a refuge, a way to transcend the immediate suffering and envision a future where divine justice and mercy would prevail.

However, upon arriving in their new environment, these refugees could find themselves facing a different set of challenges. The initial relief of reaching a safer place might soon be overshadowed by the stark realities of adjusting to a new culture, finding employment, securing housing, and navigating a complex and often unwelcoming bureaucracy. The trauma of their past experiences, coupled with the stress of adapting to an unfamiliar society, can lead to feelings of isolation, frustration, and despair.

In this context, some refugees might turn to alcohol as a means of coping. Alcohol, easily accessible and socially acceptable in many cultures, provides a temporary escape from their distressing circumstances. It numbs the pain, eases anxiety, and offers a brief respite from the harshness of their reality. This reliance on alcohol as a coping mechanism mirrors their previous dependence on religious faith but with significant differences in impact and outcome.

While religious faith often brings a sense of purpose and community, alcohol can lead to further alienation and health issues. The shift from a spiritual to a chemical form of solace underscores a more profound irony: in seeking refuge from their old lives, refugees might inadvertently adopt a new form of dependency that ultimately hinders their ability to integrate and thrive in their new environment fully. The escape provided by alcohol is fleeting and comes with consequences that can exacerbate their challenges, such as addiction, deteriorating health, and strained relationships.

This situation highlights a broader issue about the nature of coping mechanisms and the need for sustainable, healthy ways to manage life's difficulties. It calls for a comprehensive approach to refugee support that addresses not only immediate needs like shelter and employment but also provides psychological and social support to help them navigate their new lives. Programs that foster community integration, mental health services, and opportunities for meaningful engagement can help refugees build resilience and find healthier ways to cope with their experiences.

Ultimately, this irony reminds us of the complex interplay between culture, coping mechanisms, and human resilience. It underscores the importance of addressing the root causes of suffering and providing holistic support to those in need, ensuring their journey towards a better life does not lead them into new forms of despair.

Chapter 11

Beauty in God's creation – and lessons they teach us.

'Split a piece of wood; I am there. Lift up the stone, and you will find me there'.

Gospel of Thomas verse 77 [21]

I've always found it intriguing to ponder the humour God might have infused into the creatures we keep as companions, particularly cats and dogs. Dogs, those loyal and affectionate creatures, embody the essence of unconditional love. They don't love us for the food or shelter we offer; their devotion stems purely from the bond they share with us as their owners. This unwavering loyalty extends even to those without homes, where a dog will faithfully stand by its homeless owner, regardless of their hardships together. The connection between a dog and its owner is profound. In the adoring gaze of those canine eyes, we see a reflection of our significance in their world. Dogs convey with every glance, "You are my everything" and "You are the centre of my universe." Their love knows no bounds, transcending material comforts and circumstances.

Conversely, cats' aloof demeanour contrasts starkly with dogs' unwavering devotion. They regard us with a calm air as if to say, "You're mildly interesting, I suppose", or "I tolerate your presence, but remember, I am in charge." While dogs elevate us to the status of idols, cats constantly remind us of our humility. Dogs uplift us with boundless affection in this dynamic, while cats ground us with their independent spirit. It's as if God has woven a tapestry of irony into the fabric of our lives through these beloved pets, each playing a unique role in teaching us about love, loyalty, and the beauty of companionship.

During our weekly waste collection rounds, my colleague and I are treated to a delightful array of encounters with the wildlife that shares our neighbourhood. Among these creatures, squirrels stand out as particularly intriguing companions, each offering its lesson in the art of living in the moment. It's a common sight for us to pause in our duties and share a light-hearted moment as we observe a squirrel darting across our path or perched atop a fence, seemingly unfazed by our presence. In these fleeting moments, we can't help but marvel at the agility and resourcefulness of these bushy-tailed creatures. Indeed, squirrels epitomize the essence of seizing the present moment. While it's true that they dedicate much of their time to preparing for the winter months, diligently stashing away food for the colder seasons, what strikes me most is their unwavering focus on immediate tasks. Regardless of weather conditions or other obstacles, squirrels never procrastinate their foraging activities. They exhibit a remarkable awareness of the here and now, gathering nuts and seeds efficiently and purposely, wasting no time making the most of nature's bounty.

Moreover, as they go about their daily search for sustenance, squirrels remain vigilant to potential dangers lurking in their surroundings. Their keen senses and quick reflexes constantly remind them to stay alert and mindful of the present moment, even amid routine activities.

But the most endearing lesson squirrels impart is the importance of joy and playfulness in life. Watching two squirrels engage in a playful chase up a tree, their tails flicking with excitement is a poignant reminder that life is about more than work and survival. It's a reminder to embrace moments of spontaneity and whimsy, to nurture our sense of wonder and delight in the world around us. In the company of squirrels, we find teachers of mindfulness and resourcefulness and ambassadors of joy and celebration. Their presence is a gentle reminder to savour each moment, cherish the simple pleasures, and find a balance between life's responsibilities and the joys of living.

The badger is a fascinating nocturnal creature that we often encounter, albeit in unfortunate circumstances, as they are usually found dead on the roadside after being struck by cars. Despite their elusive nature, there's much to be learned from these animals. Despite weighing less than 20 kilograms, badgers can ward off larger predators like bears and wolves. Their ability to defend themselves is remarkable, yet they prefer to avoid confrontation by hunting at night. This behaviour is a valuable lesson: even when possessing strength, it's often wiser to use only when necessary. In a world that sometimes glorifies aggression and domination, the badger's example reminds us of the strength found in restraint.

Furthermore, an additional attractive trait of badgers is their practice of passing down their burrows to future generations. Rather than each badger digging its new burrow, they leave their homes as legacies for their descendants. This behaviour serves as a contrast to our throwaway society and its focus on immediate gratification. If we learn from badgers how to plan for the future and care for what we have, we could foster a culture of sustainability. By valuing and preserving resources for the next generation, we could have a profoundly positive impact on our environment.

Dogs have the greatest affection for binmen among all the animals we encounter daily. Admittedly, there are a few dogs that I am thankful to be separated from by a sturdy gate or high wall. However, more often than not, these dogs are overjoyed to see us. Our driver keeps a fresh supply of dog treats in the cabin and is always eager to share them with the canine friends we encounter along our route. It's clear that these dogs know precisely when we're coming and get extremely excited when our driver steps out to hand out the treats.

These furry friends provide me with a great deal of reflection. I often wonder if the world would experience less anger, depression, and mental health issues if we adopted the positive outlook of dogs. Dogs teach us to find contentment in the simple pleasures of everyday life. They derive immense joy from playing catch with a ball, bouncing through freshly fallen snow, chasing their tails, or being petted. There are days when we reluctantly get out of bed, dreading the workday or the chores that await us.

In contrast, a dog awakens with boundless enthusiasm, ready to embrace whatever the new day brings. The most profound lesson dogs teach us is the power of forgiveness and the art of letting go. Any dog owner who has scolded their pet will recognize the look of longing for reconciliation when all is forgiven and harmony is restored. Despite any annoyance or reprimand, dogs are quick to forgive and eager to move on. This ability to forgive and forget, a trait we could all benefit from, is a powerful lesson we can learn from our canine companions.

As I work in rural areas, I am afforded more time in the cab, allowing me to reflect deeply. During our travels, I am constantly in awe of the beautiful creatures we encounter, from the serene sheep in the paddock at South Kelsey to the majestic peacocks at Waddingham. These encounters with nature are enlightening as many creatures move leisurely, fully embracing the present moment and finding joy in life's simple pleasures. It's a humbling reminder that, as humans, we often become so absorbed in our hurried routines that we neglect to slow down and appreciate the beauty surrounding us. How frequently do we pause, approach a delicate rose, and breathe in its exquisite fragrance? These instances are poignant reminders that God has intricately woven profound lessons into the fabric of nature, offering us insights into how to live honestly and what is of fundamental significance. When I gaze at the countryside, I am continuously captivated by the profound wisdom and intricate designs that reflect God's creativity. The animals, from the tiniest insects to the largest mammals, each play their role in this complicated web of life. Their behaviours and interactions reflect a natural order and balance, a testament to a

Creator who values harmony and cooperation. Watching a bird build its nest or a deer graze peacefully in a meadow, we see lessons of care, perseverance, and the gentle rhythms of life that God has set in motion. Rural landscapes' rich tapestry of diverse features and intricate patterns is a vibrant testament to the divine's profound wisdom and boundless creativity. Every facet of the natural world showcases exquisite artistry that guides us to marvel at the intricacy and beauty of our surroundings and acknowledge the presence of the Creator in every detail.

Chapter 12

Waste is simply waste; it's all the same.

'God loves each of us as if there were only one of us'.

Saint Augustine [22]

I thought I would also share with you, the reader, some of the inner workings of how the council handles waste disposal in Lincolnshire. This will give you a better understanding of the complexities and challenges of ensuring timely and efficient waste collection services. Occasionally, we receive complaints about not arriving on time for weekly waste collections. While we understand the frustration these delays can cause, rest assured that we are doing our utmost to be punctual and provide the best service possible. Our team, typically consisting of two or three members, is focused on more than just collecting your waste. Our operations are far more extensive and involve various tasks and responsibilities. One of the busiest days in our schedule is Friday when our team visits over a thousand homes. This requires meticulous planning and coordination to complete all scheduled collections. Despite our best efforts, factors beyond our control can cause delays. For instance, vehicle breakdowns are an occasional but inevitable challenge that can disrupt our schedule. In addition, navigating through busy roads, especially during peak hours, can significantly slow down our progress. Our waste collection vehicles are maintained regularly to minimize the risk of breakdowns, and we plan our routes carefully to avoid the busiest roads whenever possible. However, unexpected situations such as road closures, traffic accidents, and inclement weather can also contribute to delays.

In addition, I was somewhat reluctant to share a big secret with you; however, I feel that the truth needs telling – all your waste goes to the same place. Whether it is the Waitrose Slow Cooked Lamb Kleftico, deliciously described as slow-cooked lamb shoulder on the bone with a lemon, garlic, and rosemary marinade, or the Iceland Chicken Curry with Rice microwave meal, they all end up together in the back of the bin lorry. To add another considerable reveal, everything gets dumped together regardless of whether we are tipping our bin lorries at the Lincoln incinerator or the council waste station at Gainsborough. This might be a surprise, given the variety of waste and the range of supermarkets and stores from which it originates. For some ludicrous reason, the council refuses to employ binmen to sort the waste into neat heaps based on their origin, such as Waitrose, Home Bargains, M&S, Tesco, Iceland, and Aldi groupings. We have tried to convince the council about the potential benefits of sorting waste this way. However, council bosses will not have it. They argue that the logistical challenges and additional costs associated with such sorting are prohibitive.

They also point out that the current waste management infrastructure is designed to handle mixed waste efficiently, directing it all to incineration for energy recovery. Despite our best efforts, the council remains steadfast in its approach. They maintain that the focus should be on improving overall waste management systems and public education on waste reduction and recycling rather than on the specific sorting of waste by store origin. So, for now, whether your waste comes from a high-end grocery store or a budget supermarket, it all ends up in the same place, processed together in our waste management facilities. So when I am standing at the back of the bin lorry, I have to force myself to watch how all the waste gets treated equally, all having the same eventuality; waste is simply waste; it's all the same. Although the bin lorry is packed with various items, to me, the binman, it is just waste.

Being who I am, I can't help but take this simple matter and ponder it deeper. I look at all humans and wonder if God views us all the same. Please understand me; I'm not suggesting God sees us as rubbish. However, I question whether Saint Augustine was right when he said, "God loves each of us as if there were only one of us." You'll get different answers to this question depending on whom you ask. It also yields different answers when considered through the lens of history. Thousands of years ago, the Egyptians believed they were an elite people, leading them to enslave the Jews and use them to build their pyramids and other structures. A hundred years ago, God-fearing Christian men and women felt justified in enslaving African men and women to work on cotton plantations in America. I grew up in South Africa, where non-white people often believed that God was the God of the white man. My black brothers would observe how the white man enjoyed all the luxuries and assume that God was only taking care of the white minority. What else could explain why black people were kept subservient? This idea is so deeply ingrained that on our last visit to South

Africa, a black petrol attendant asked my wife to pray for him because he had an upset stomach. We need to ask ourselves what has caused this poor man to believe that he didn't have the right to pray to God for assistance and needed a white woman to pray on his behalf.

From a young age, I was raised as a Christian and taught that Christians were God's chosen people. This belief was instilled in me through religious teachings and community practices. However, what's particularly interesting is that when you talk to a Catholic, Baptist, Mormon, or a member of one of the new Evangelical churches - all of whom are Christians - they all believe that they are God's chosen ones and that everyone else is not. If they didn't hold this belief, why doesn't a Jehovah's Witness attend services at the local Methodist church? Each denomination believes in its unique relationship with God, a conviction that separates them from others, even within the broader Christian faith.

This sense of being uniquely chosen is not confined to Christianity. Jewish believers and Islamic adherents also firmly believe that they are God's chosen people. Each religion instils in its followers a belief in their special status and direct favour from God. This belief often extends to the idea that God blesses them while others are not. For instance, many people speak of being blessed by God, implying a special divine favour. But what does this mean for those who do not share their faith? Are they not blessed by God? In making such exclusive claims, religion has caused considerable harm. It fosters divisions and a sense of superiority among different groups. How often have you heard someone say God has blessed them? This assertion carries the implicit message that others, perhaps those of different faiths or none at all, are not similarly blessed. This kind of thinking can lead to exclusion and a lack of empathy for those outside one's religious community. However, I am reminded of the words of Jesus in the Bible: "… that you may prove yourselves to be sons of your

Father who is in heaven; for He causes His sun to rise on the evil and the good and sends rain on the righteous and the unrighteous" (Matthew 5:45, NASB). [23] This verse suggests a more inclusive view of divine love and blessing, one that extends beyond the boundaries of any single religious group. It emphasizes that God's grace and provision are available to all, regardless of their moral standing or religious affiliation. While many spiritual traditions claim exclusive favour with God, it is essential to recognize the broader, more inclusive message that divine love and blessings are meant for everyone.

While I still identify as a Christian, I strive to seek truth by observing the world that God has created around me. During my journeys, I often encounter grazing paddocks where cows and horses are kept. What strikes me is that regardless of the differences among the cows, whether in their colour or breed, they all have the same vegetation to feed on. It's as if God doesn't favour one type of cow over another; each has access to the same resources. I highly doubt that a cow would turn to its fellow and claim to have been blessed with an incredibly lush patch of grass by God. Similarly, when passing the horse farms between Lea Fields Crematorium and Knaith, I see the same fairness extended to these beautiful animals, regardless of their breed or colour. It's a thought-provoking realization that reflects the impartiality of God's provision.

Reflecting on how God treats everyone and everything under heaven inspires me to do the same. I strive to treat all people and animals without favouritism. The ancient Chinese philosophers understood this wisdom well when they said:

The sage is like heaven and earth;

To him, none are especially dear,

Nor is there anyone he disfavours.

He gives and gives, without condition' offering his treasures to everyone.

(Tao Te Ching, 5thverse). [24]

I am fully aware that there is significant suffering and injustice in the world. However, I do not hold God responsible for this. What I find particularly distressing is when religious individuals lead opulent lifestyles, refuse to share their resources, and then blame God for withholding His goodness from the less fortunate. This behaviour strikes me as especially cruel and hypocritical. The reason so many people go hungry today is not because they are lazy or refuse to work, and indeed, not because God refuses to meet their needs. Instead, it is because the wealthy often hoard their resources, sell them at exorbitant prices, and disregard the suffering of the poor. If we all viewed those around us as equals and did not feel compelled to accumulate more and better possessions but instead were willing to share what we have, how could there be hunger and poverty in our world?

The problem lies not in divine neglect but in human greed and selfishness. Many of the world's resources are concentrated in the hands of a few, who prioritize their wealth over the well-being of others. This disparity is perpetuated by a lack of empathy and a failure to recognize our shared humanity. Imagine a world where everyone embraced the principle of equality and generosity. If we all committed to ensuring that no one went without, prioritizing communal well-being over personal gain would drastically diminish hunger and poverty. This shift in perspective would lead to a more just and compassionate society, where resources are distributed more equitably and the needs of the less fortunate are met. The root cause of much of the world's suffering is not a lack of divine provision but a failure in human stewardship. By fostering a culture of sharing and caring, we can address these injustices and create a world where everyone has the opportunity to thrive.

So, the next time you remove your bin for collection, remember that all waste is ultimately waste, regardless of its source. However, I encourage you to also reflect on the deeper meanings of life. Consider how we are all of equal value, as we are all children of God. When you place your bin on the curb, please take a moment to ponder the unity and equality that we share as human beings. Just as all types of waste end up in the same place, our differences in status, wealth, or background do not change our intrinsic worth. We are all connected by our shared humanity and our shared divine heritage. Think about how this perspective can influence your actions and interactions. Recognizing that everyone is of equal value makes you more inclined to treat others with kindness, respect, and compassion. This simple reflection can remind you to live out these values daily, fostering a sense of community and mutual care. In essence, as you handle the mundane task of taking out the trash, let it prompt a moment of contemplation about life's more profound truths. Embrace the idea that we are all equally valuable and beloved in the eyes of God, and let this understanding guide you in your relationships and actions.

Chapter 13

Navigating the Streets with Dyspraxia.

(A return to Nettleham)

'When I discover who I am, then I will be free'.

Ralp Ellison [25]

As I reflect on the past year, I find it quite ironic that my journey began in Nettleham, and now, a year later, it is concluding in the same place. The past year has been full of ups and downs, and returning to this town stirred up mixed emotions within me. I must confess that I was apprehensive about returning here, considering it's the place that shattered my confidence on my first day. Despite my initial fears, I persevered and honed my skills while working across the West Lindsey district. Each day brought improvement, but I knew I would eventually have to confront my deepest fears. Finally, that day arrived, and I could face and overcome the "monster in the closet" that had been haunting me.

However, nothing is quite simple when learning a new skill. When I started working as a binman, I quickly learned that one of the job rituals was receiving an official nickname from my fellow crew members. To my chagrin, I was dubbed 'Satnav', a moniker highlighting my remarkable inability to navigate even the most straightforward routes. Despite my best efforts, my sense of direction was abysmal, and my colleagues found great amusement in my perpetual confusion. Upon joining my bin round, our driver kindly informed me that it would take approximately a month to become acquainted with the route. However, no amount of time would remedy my navigational challenges, to everyone's surprise, including my own. Even after seven months of undertaking the same route week after week, I continued to astound my teammates with my consistent ability to veer off course. Initially, my frequent wrong turns and repeated excursions down familiar streets likely frustrated my coworkers, causing delays and wasting time. However, as time passed, my colleagues adopted a light-hearted approach, choosing to sit back and enjoy a good-natured chuckle while patiently awaiting my realization of another blunder. It has become a running joke among us, and these moments have fostered a sense of camaraderie and amusement during our shifts.

The reason for my difficulties is that I have dyspraxia, also known as developmental coordination disorder (DCD). This neurological condition impairs the ability to plan and execute motor tasks. Individuals with dyspraxia often struggle with coordination and movement, which impacts daily activities and learning. For me, it has also resulted in a poor sense of direction.

From a very early age, it was clear that things didn't come as quickly to me as they did to other children.

Learning new skills always required much more effort on my part compared to my friends and siblings. Simple activities like bike riding, dancing, swimming, and participating in coordinated sports and games were particularly challenging. While my siblings seemed to glide through the water effortlessly, I felt like a cat desperately trying to swim. My brothers excelled at ball games, but I often found myself struggling to keep up, and on some occasions, I even tripped over my feet.

Consequently, I've had my fair share of broken bones, including multiple instances of breaking my arm and collarbone. The most recent mishap occurred while I was playing squash and accidentally ran straight into a glass wall. Unfortunately, such challenges were not correctly identified or diagnosed during my upbringing. As a result, I was often unfairly labelled as clumsy or unintelligent. Had my condition been recognized earlier, I might have received the necessary support and assistance during my formative years. However, that was not the case at the time.

Thankfully, when I attended university, I found the support that eventually led to a life-changing diagnosis. I vividly recall the day I received my diagnosis and the overwhelming sense of relief that washed over me. Finally, understanding that my struggles were not due to personal shortcomings but rather a neurological condition beyond my control, I cried tears of relief. It was an awakening— a moment of understanding my true self for the first time. The realization that I wasn't useless or stupid but was dealing with a neurological condition was incredibly freeing. It's as if a weight had been lifted off my shoulders. Understanding and accepting myself in this new light was like breaking free from chains that had confined me for so long. As I began comprehending the root of my challenges, I came across the phrase, "When I discover who I am, then I will be free." [1] This resonated with me on a deep level. It became clear that true personal freedom can only be achieved through self-discovery and understanding.

Realizing that I had dyspraxia was a significant moment for me. It made me recognize that I encountered specific challenges that were unique to me. Despite putting in a lot of effort, I came to terms with the fact that there were some tasks that I would struggle with and would take time to master. This journey of self-discovery was pivotal in helping me understand that while external influences and societal expectations do exist, there are certain things that I cannot excel at. Through deep introspection, I could identify my strengths and weaknesses, and this awareness played a crucial role in alleviating the self-doubt and insecurities I had been carrying. Understanding my true self has given me a sense of resilience. It has equipped me to face life's challenges and setbacks more confidently. As a result, I no longer feel constrained by what I cannot comprehend; instead, I'm learning to embrace my authentic self and make proper choices rather than succumbing to external pressures. One of the most valuable aspects of this journey has been the spiritual freedom I've gained – a more profound sense of peace and contentment, along with an understanding of my purpose in the world and the universe. Furthermore, I've come to realize that the process of self-discovery often leads to uncovering one's passions and life's purpose. Aligning my actions with my purpose has brought a profound sense of meaning and direction, ultimately enhancing my overall sense of freedom.

I am always amazed by how quickly my colleagues in refuse collection learn the intricacies of our trade. Sometimes, I jokingly tease them about their seemingly effortless skill in manoeuvring the bins. Despite handling tens of thousands of bins over time, I still need help with coordination and experience occasional delays. This challenge becomes more demanding during black bin weeks, when we have to handle bins of three different sizes, adding another level of complexity to the task. Sadly, there have been a couple of instances where the contents of my bins spilled out onto the road, prompting gentle reminders from my coworkers that the idea is to get the rubbish into the back of the lorry and not all over the street.

When encouraging new team members, I emphasize that they can excel in this role with practice. From my experiences, I've learned that resilience is critical. Even when faced with daunting challenges, perseverance and dedication are crucial for improvement. I could understand anyone with dyspraxia giving up and saying, 'I cannot do this job, as it is just too hard'. However, despite mountain-like obstacles, individuals can accomplish anything they set their minds on. If you want to achieve something, never let anyone tell you that you are not good enough or that you should do something else with your time. If someone in your life is constantly putting you down, try and spend less time in their company, even if you do not give them your energy or allow them to get inside your mind.

The American motivational speaker Zig Ziglar once said, "Your attitude, not your aptitude, will determine your altitude." [26] This means that having a positive and determined attitude can propel a person to achieve great heights, regardless of their initial skill level. It's a reminder that perseverance, resilience, and taking proactive steps can often lead to success more effectively than talent alone. My favourite quote from Zig Ziglar is, "Remember, a failure is an event, not a person." [27] This implies that making mistakes or facing failure is only a temporary setback and does not define the person as a failure. We should use our failures as learning experiences and an opportunity to grow and improve on our way to our goals, never accepting defeat.

Always believe that greatness lies within you, waiting to be unleashed from whatever holds it back. You possess the talent, strength, and potential to achieve extraordinary things deep inside. Trust in your abilities and know that you can reach incredible heights. Every challenge you face, and every obstacle you overcome brings you one step closer to uncovering your true potential.

Be the best version of yourself. Continuously strive for self-improvement and growth, recognizing that each day presents an opportunity to become better than you were the day before. Embrace your unique qualities and talents and let them shine. Authenticity is powerful; let the world see the real you, with all your strengths and imperfections. By being genuine, you inspire others and create meaningful connections. Never hold back from reaching your fullest potential. The journey to greatness is not always easy, and there will be times when you doubt yourself or face setbacks. However, it's crucial to persevere and maintain your belief in your capabilities. Push through the fear, the doubt, and the challenges, knowing they are merely stepping stones on your path to success. Your potential is boundless, and with determination and self-belief, you can achieve anything you want.

References

1 Ellison, R. (1952). *Invisible man.* Vintage. https://www.goodreads.com/quotes/6987-when-i-discover-who-i-am-i-ll-be-free

2 Goodreads. (2024). *Anatole France.* https://www.goodreads.com/quotes/45218-if-we-don-t-change-we-don-t-grow-if-we-don-t

3 Law, S. (2007). *The great philosophers.* Quercus. pp. 98 – 101.

4 Dyer, D. (2008). *Living the wisdom of the Tao.* Hay House. p. 41

5 Quotefancy. (2024). *Wayne W. Dyer quotes.* https://quotefancy.com/quote/932765/Wayne-W-Dyer-Know-that-success-and-inner-peace-are-your-birthright-that-you-are-a-child

6 BibleGateway. *NIV Bible Online.* (2011). https://www.biblegateway.com/passage/?search=Matthew%2018%3A3&version=NIV

7 Reuters. (2013, June 5). *Wasting food is like stealing from the poor, the pope says.* https://www.reuters.com/article/lifestyle/wasting-food-is-like-stealing-from-poor-pope-says-idUSBRE9540P2/#:~:text=%22Throwing%20awa

	y%20food%20is%20like,to%20practice%20greater%20austerity%20itself.
8	BibleGateway. *Contemporary English Version Bible Online.* https://www.biblegateway.com/passage/?search=Matthew%207%3A9-11&version=CEV
9	Dyer, D. (2008). *Living the wisdom of the Tao.* Hay House. p. 163
10	Goodreads. (2024). *John Bunyan.* https://www.goodreads.com/quotes/41980-you-have-not-lived-today-until-you-have-done-something
11	BibleGateway. *New American Standard Bible Online.* https://www.biblegateway.com/passage/?search=Matthew%206%3A2-4&version=NASB
12	BrainyQuote. (2024). *Gabrielle Bernstein Quotes.* https://www.brainyquote.com/quotes/gabrielle_bernstein_899078
13	Goodreads. (2024). *Courtney M. Privett.* https://www.goodreads.com/quotes/11560105-what-is-life-without-loss-love-without-loneliness-ecstasy-without

14   BibleGateway. *NIV Bible Online.* (2011).
      https://www.biblegateway.com/passage/?search=Ecclesiastes%203%3A11&version=NIV

15   GetInspiredSpiritually. (2021, October 9). *In Life, every gain has a corresponding loss; every loss has a ….* https://www.getinspiredspiritually.com/post/in-life-every-gain-has-a-loss-amp-every-loss-has

16   Gruen, L. (Summer 2021 Edition). The Moral Status of Animals. *The Stanford Encyclopedia of Philosophy.* https://plato.stanford.edu/entries/moral-animal/

17   BibleGateway. *NIV Bible Online.* (2011). https://www.biblegateway.com/passage/?search=Genesis%201%3A26&version=NIV

18   BibleGateway. *Contemporary English Version Bible Online.* https://www.biblegateway.com/passage/?search=Matthew%206%3A26&version=CEV

19   BibleGateway. *New American Bible (Revised Edition).* https://www.biblegateway.com/passage/?search=Matthew%2010%3A29&version=NABRE

20   Cullis, A. (2019, January 14). *Beyond Food and Alcohol: New Year with Nietzsche.* https://warwick.ac.uk/newsandevents/knowledgecentre/society/philosophy/nietzschenewyear/

21 Penguin Classics. (2021). *The Apocryphal Gospels*. Penguin Books. p. 64

22 Goodreads. (2024). *Augustine of Hippo*. https://www.goodreads.com/quotes/9316639-god-loves-each-of-us-as-if-there-were-only

23 BibleGateway. *New American Standard Bible Online*. https://www.biblegateway.com/passage/?search=Matthew%205%3A45&version=NASB

24 Dyer, D. (2008). *Living the wisdom of the Tao*. Hay House. p. 11

25 Ellison, R. (1952). *Invisible man*. Vintage. https://www.goodreads.com/quotes/6987-when-i-discover-who-i-am-i-ll-be-free

26 BrainyQuote. (2024). Zig Ziglar Quotes. https://www.brainyquote.com/quotes/zig_ziglar_381975

Printed in Great Britain
by Amazon